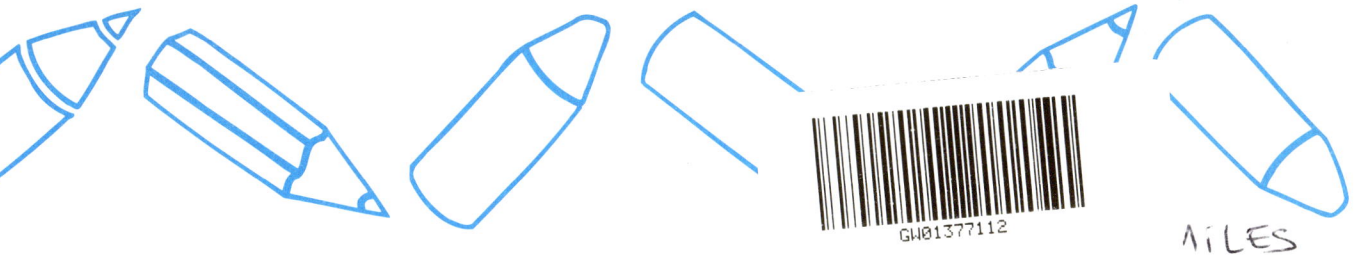

• JENNY ACKLAND

At Home with Writing

• Oxford University Press •

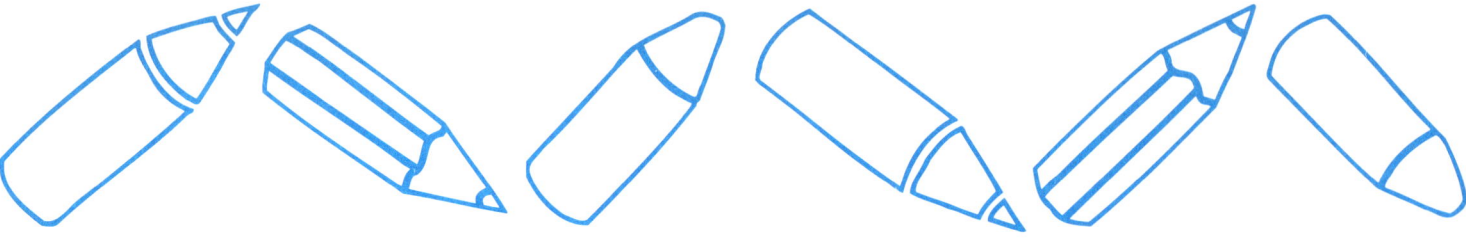

How to help your child

- Choose a quiet time to sit together, when your child is not tired or distracted.
- Work in short periods of activity, and stop as soon as your child loses concentration.
- Talk through the activities with your child, to make sure they realize that each writing movement conveys a sound or a meaning.
- Teach your child the correct pencil hold, as shown, and make sure they are sitting comfortably without the hand getting too tense.

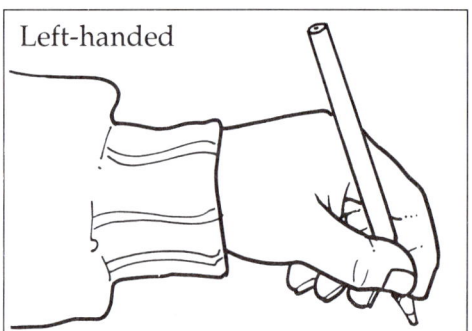
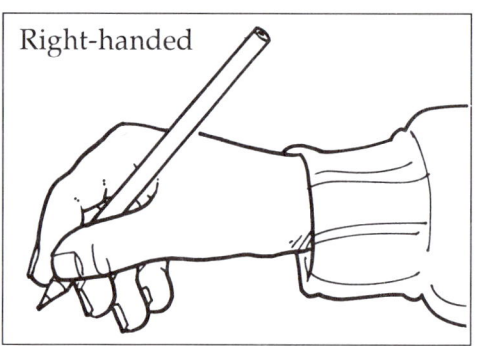

Hold the crayon or pencil between the index finger and thumb. Some children seem to need two fingers on top of the writing implement. This is quite acceptable providing the writing flow isn't inhibited. The other fingers are bent underneath the pencil to act as a cushion. The end of the pencil should rest against the curve between finger and thumb and point over the shoulder on that side.

- Don't rush past the stage of drawing patterns and colouring in, as these activities are vital for developing muscle control, hand–eye coordination, and a sense of movement.
- Letter forms come later, once the child is confident in controlling the pencil.
- Give plenty of praise and encouragement.
- Remember that the workbook should be fun for your child, as well as being educationally worthwhile.

About Writing

The process of learning to write involves all of the following skills:
- muscular control of the hand and pencil
- hand–eye coordination
- left-to-right movement
- memorizing individual letter shapes
- association of letters with sounds

Further notes on the individual sections are provided on page 48.

• CONTENTS •

Writing pathways 4–23

c, o, a, d 24–32

r, n, m 33–37

l, t 38–39

s, h 40–42

Writing practice 43–47

Notes for parents 48

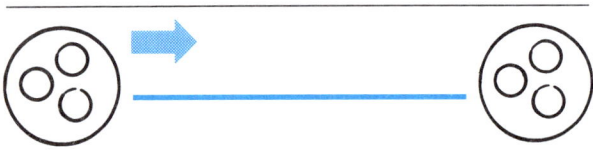

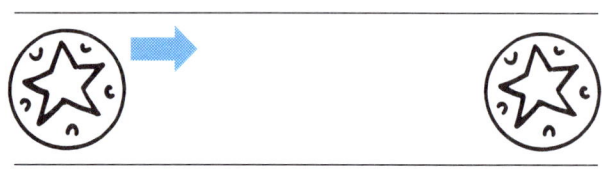

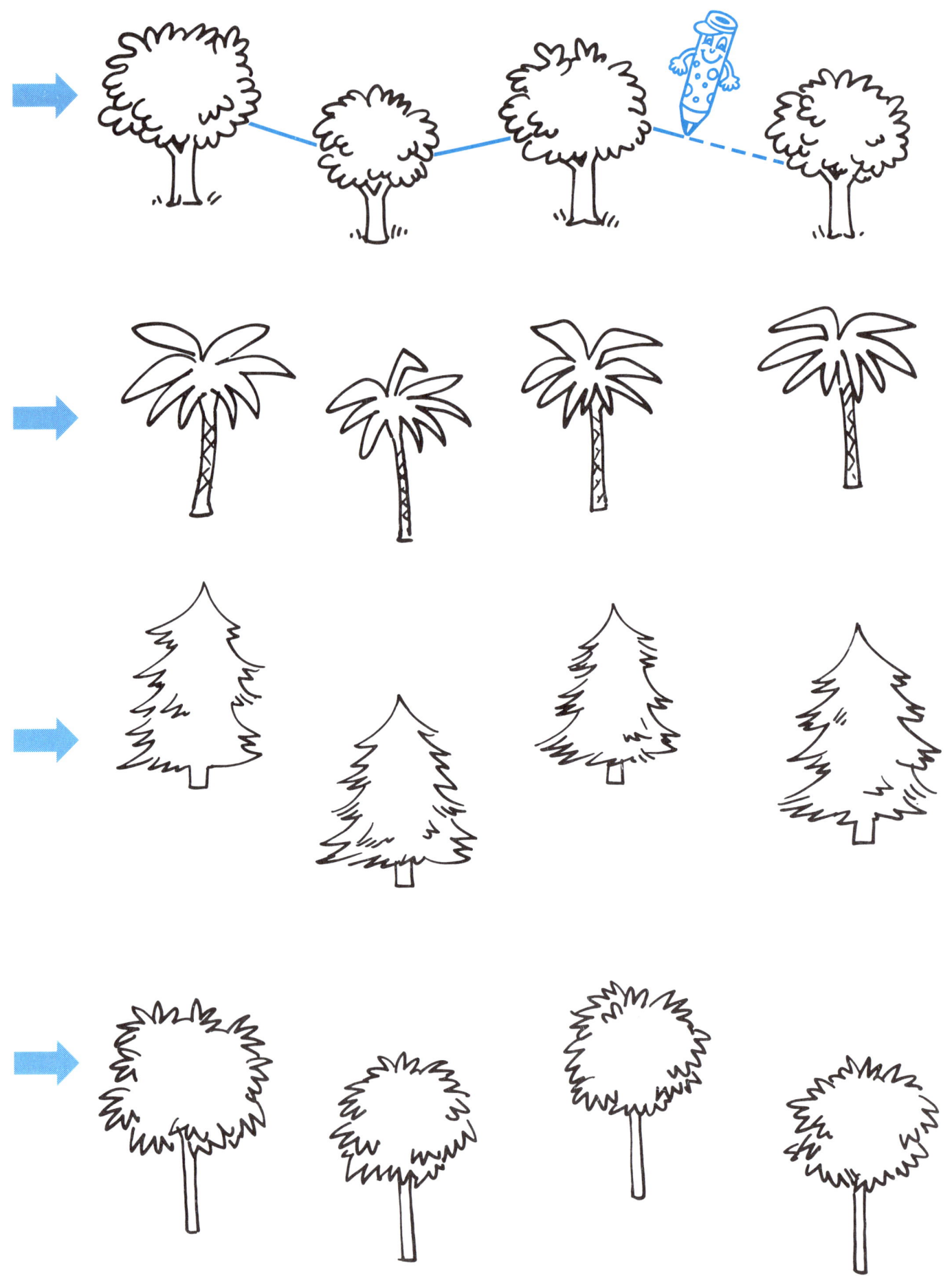

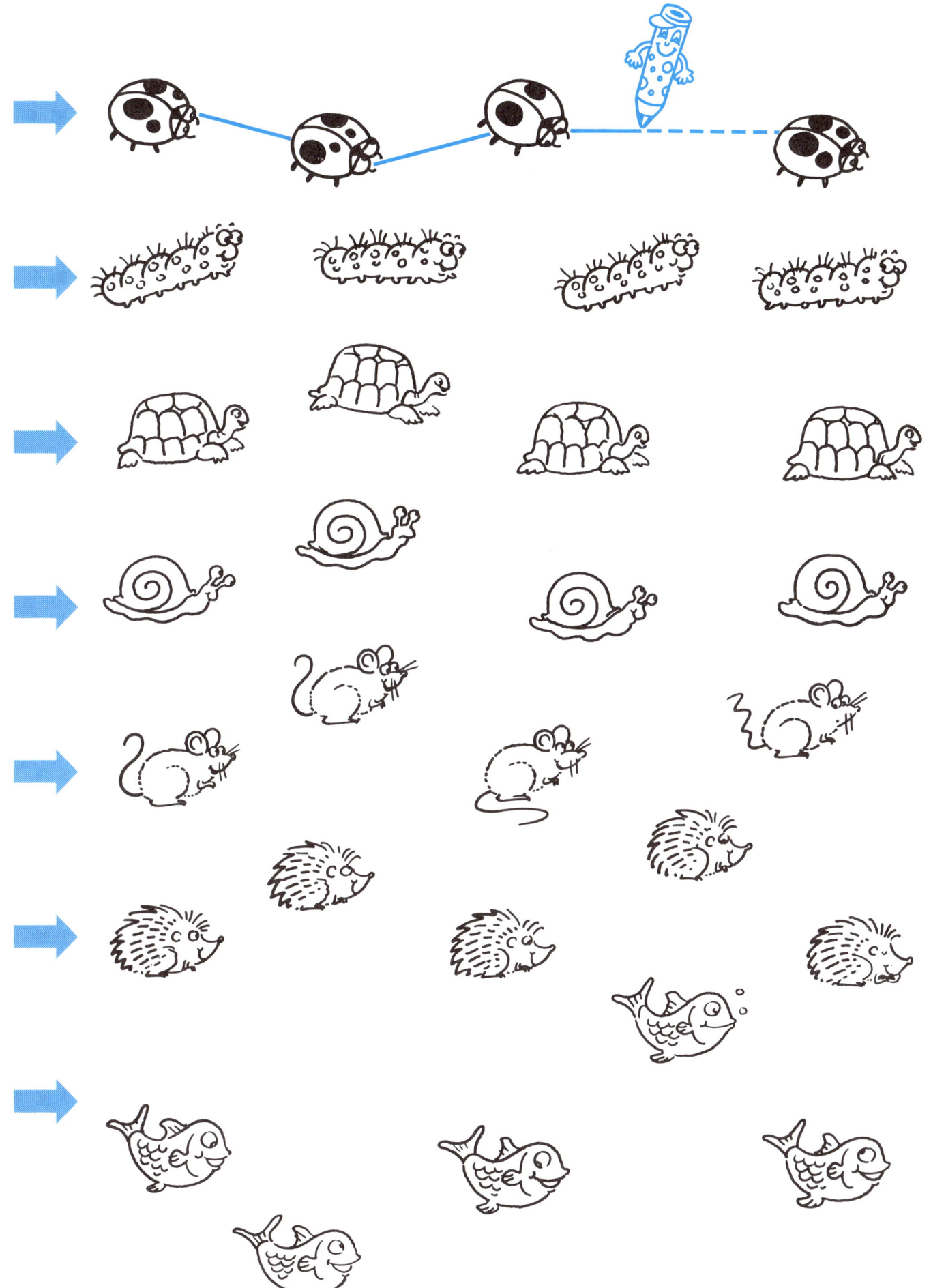

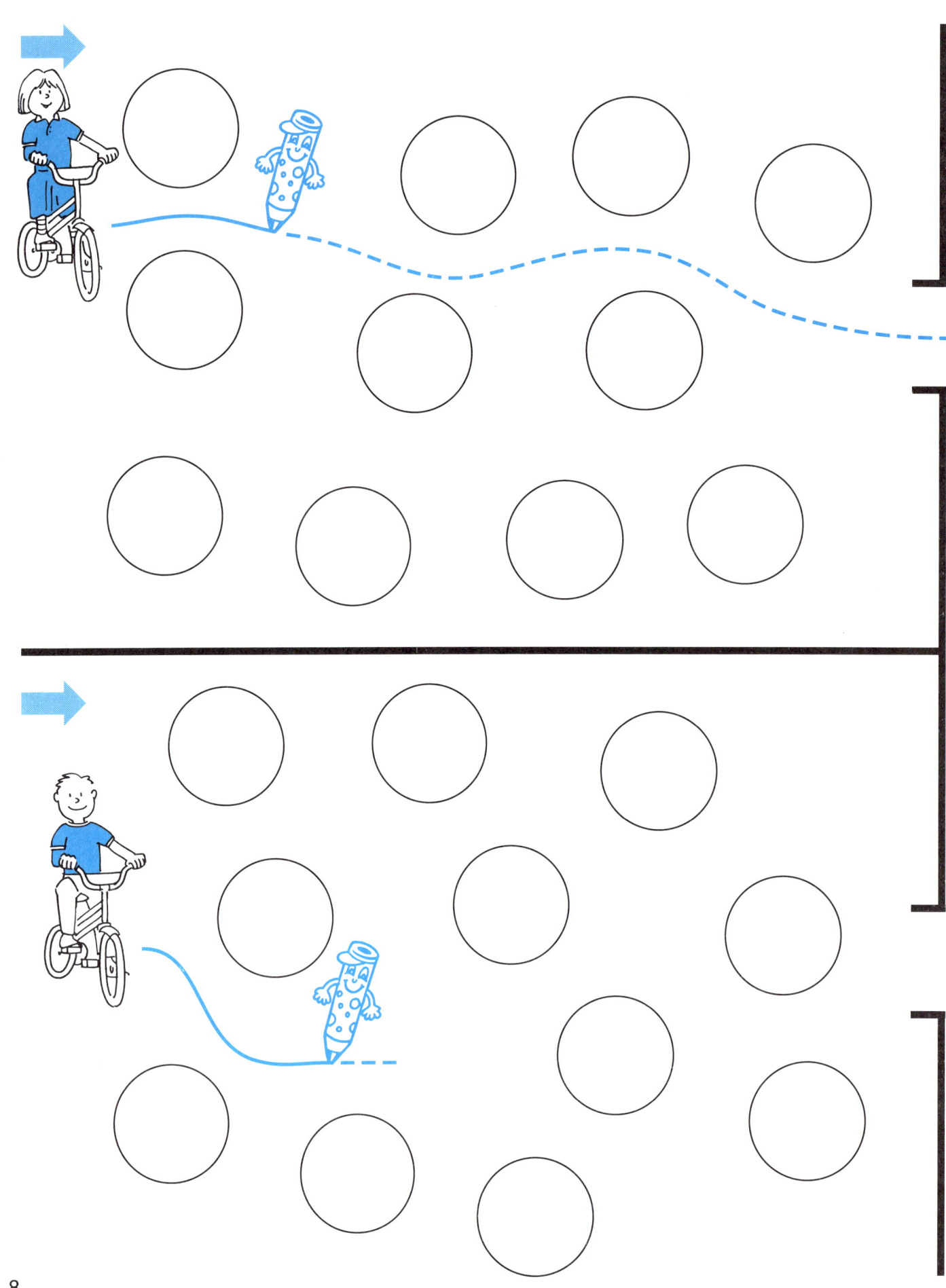

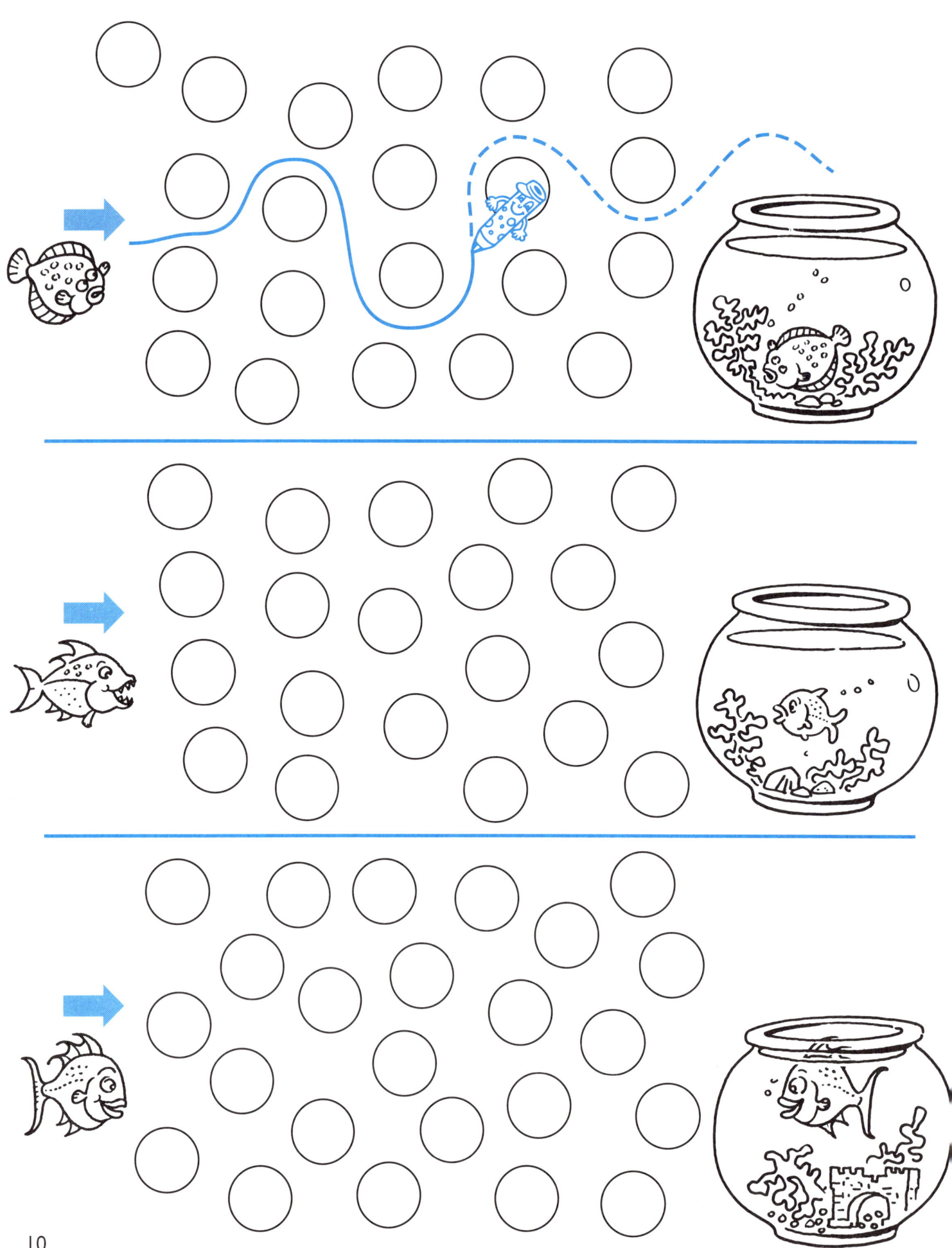

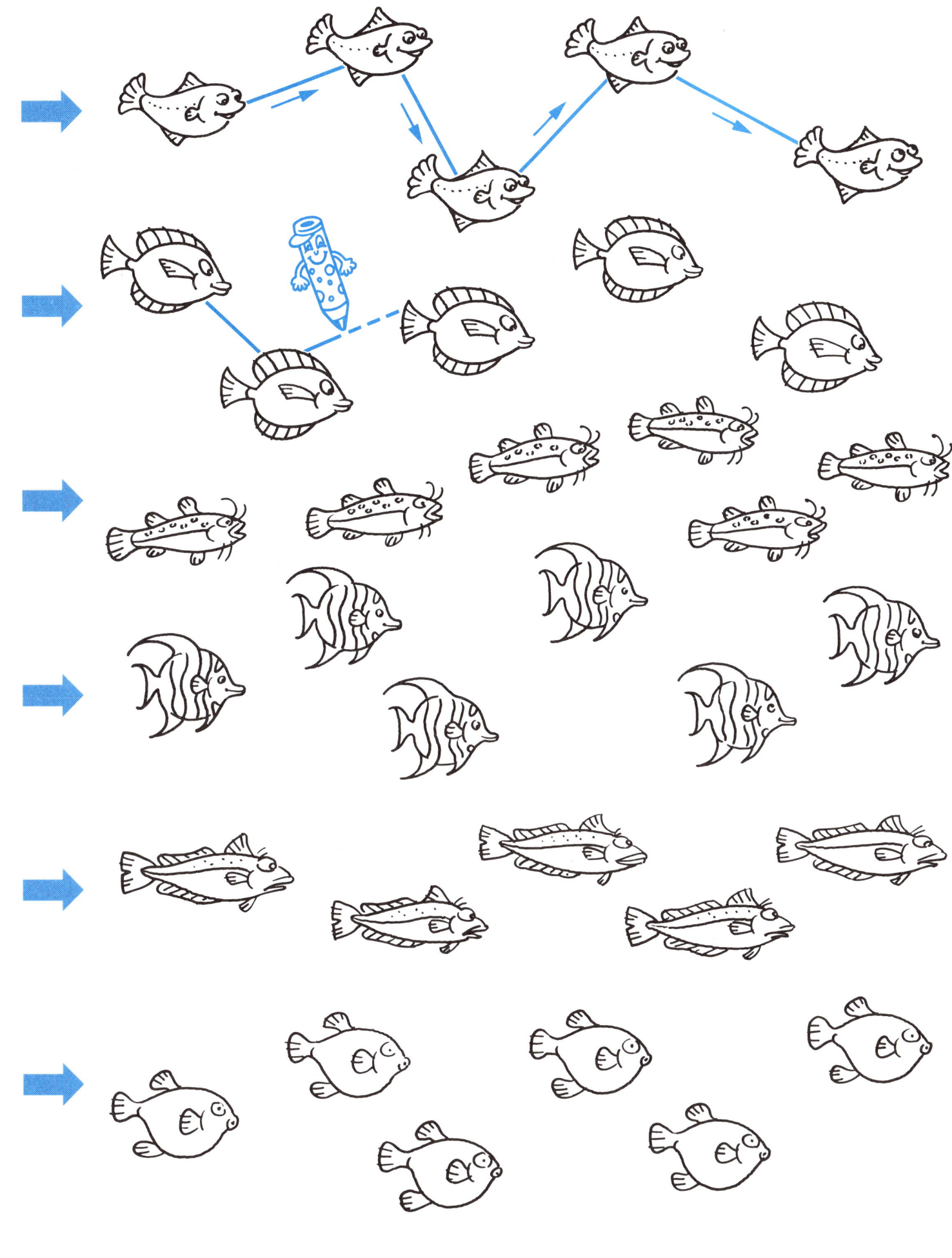

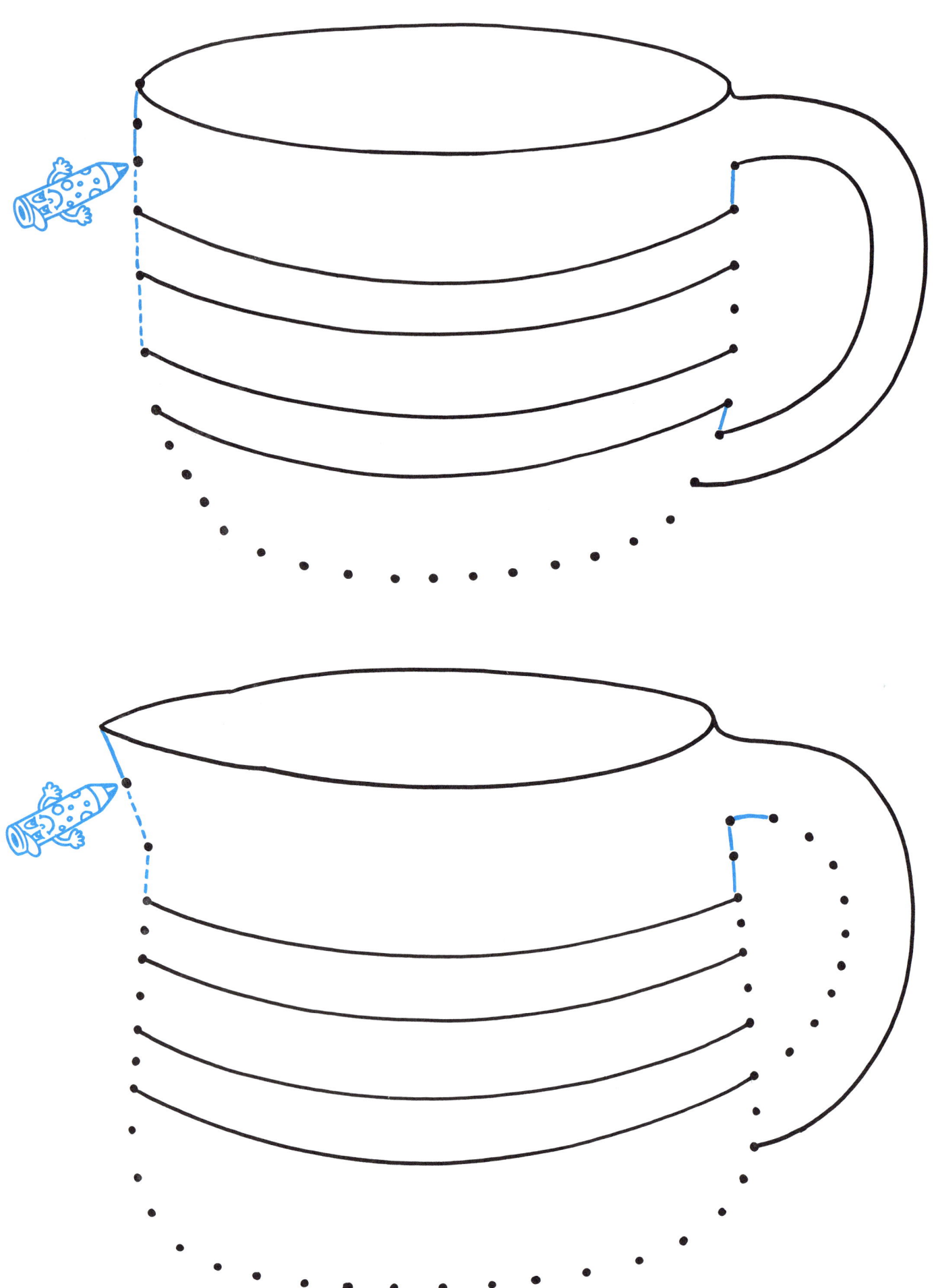

Join up the same

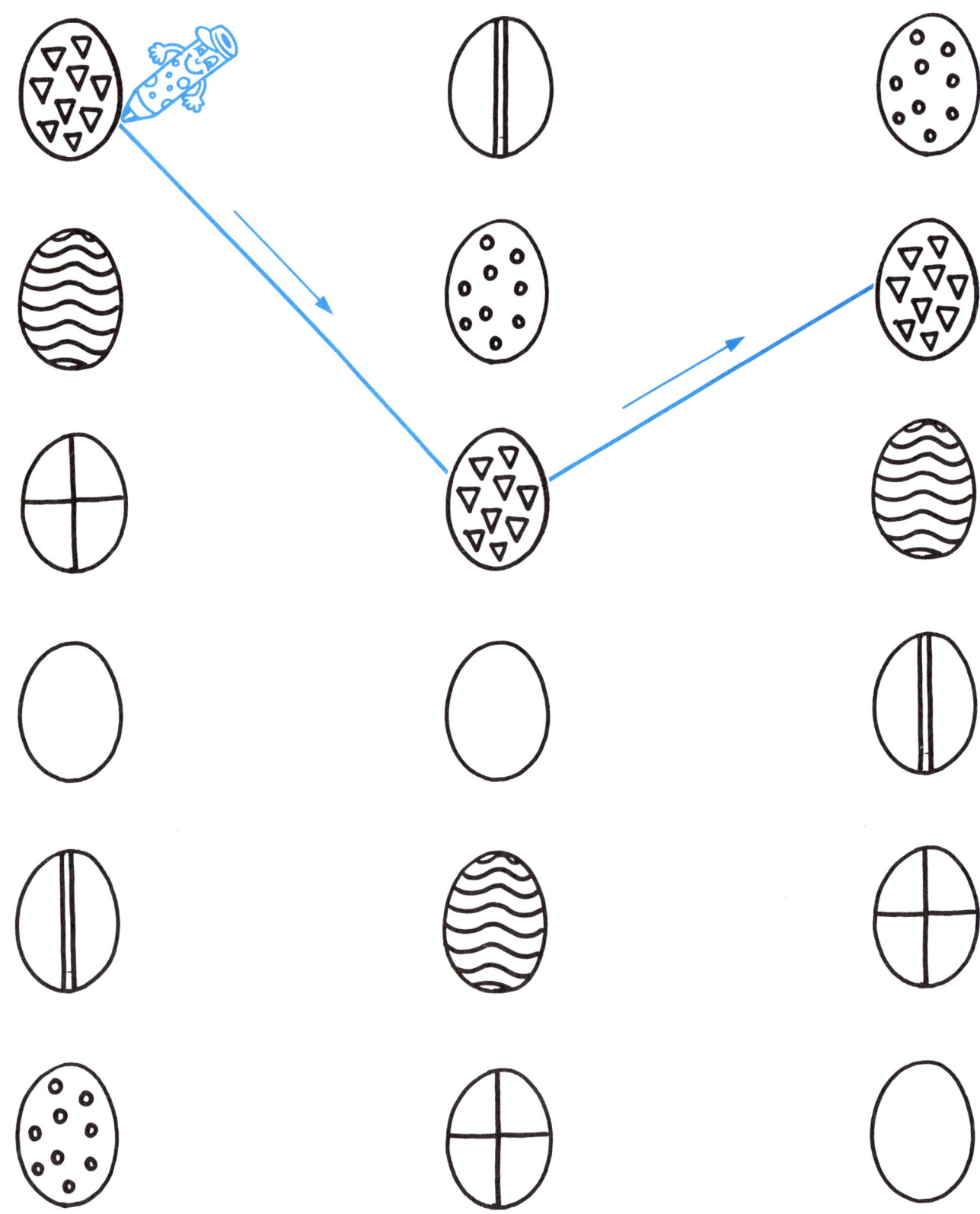

Join up the same

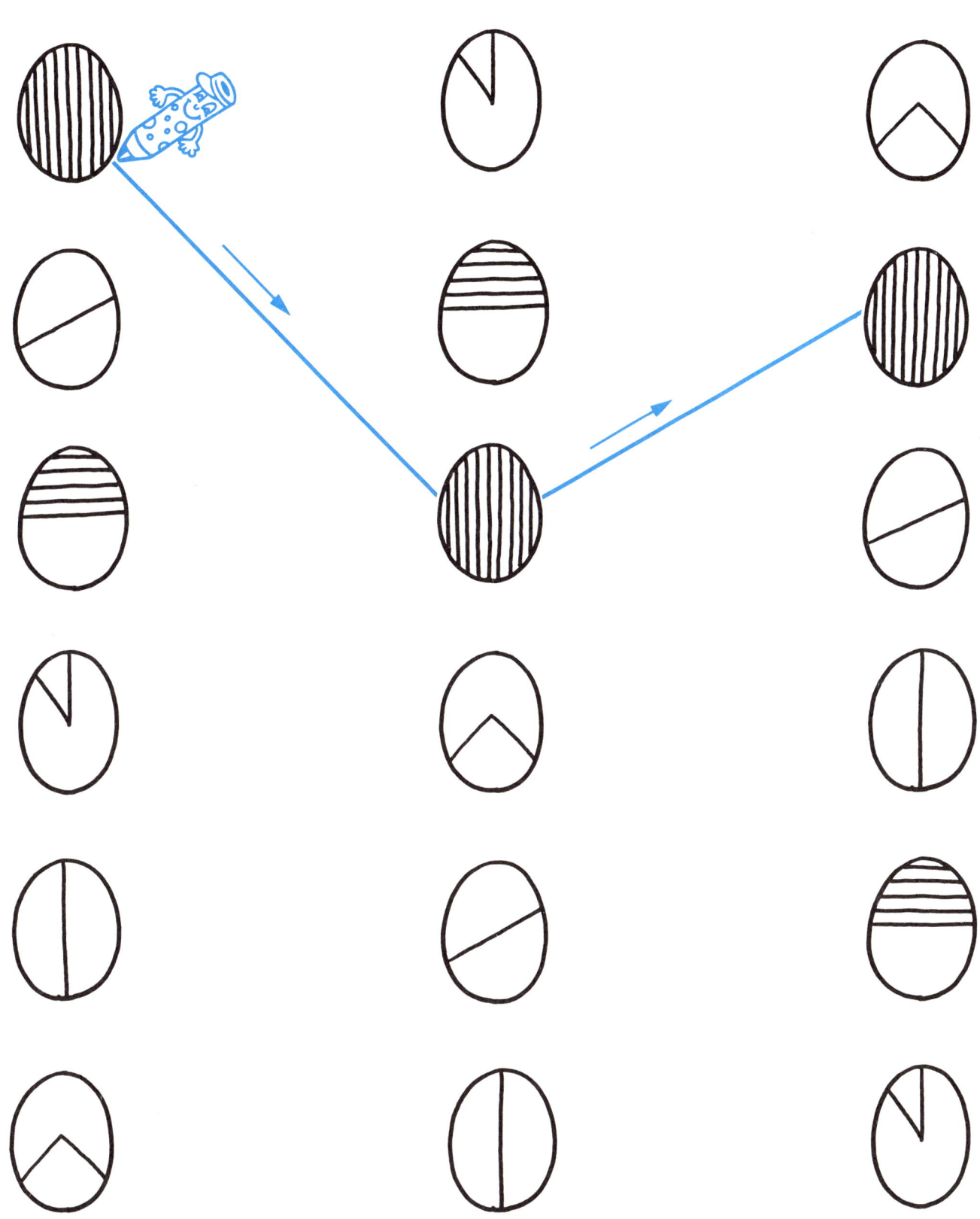

blue

red

red

green

blue
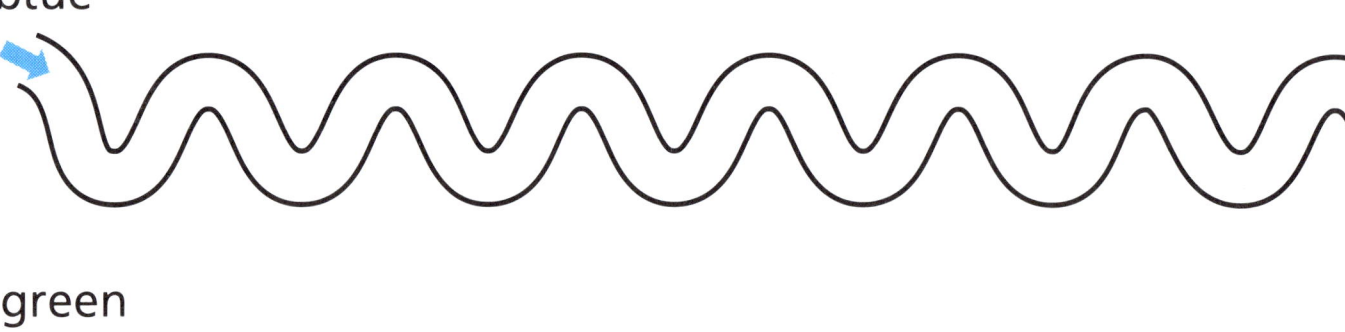

green
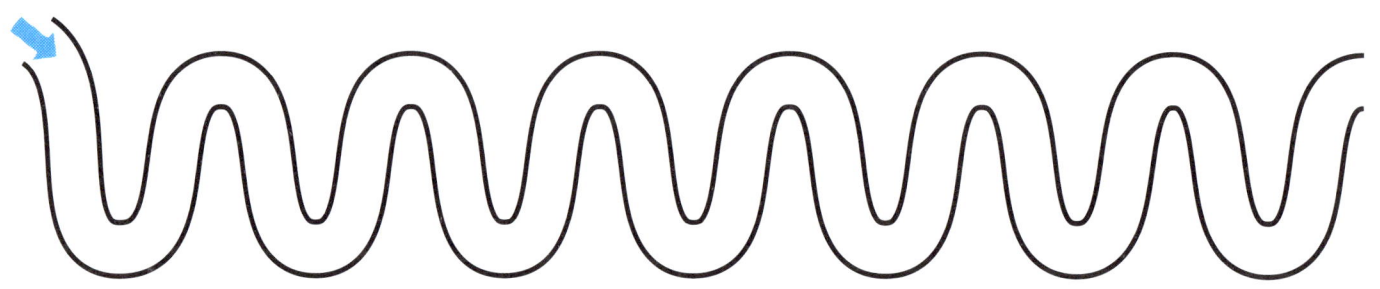

16

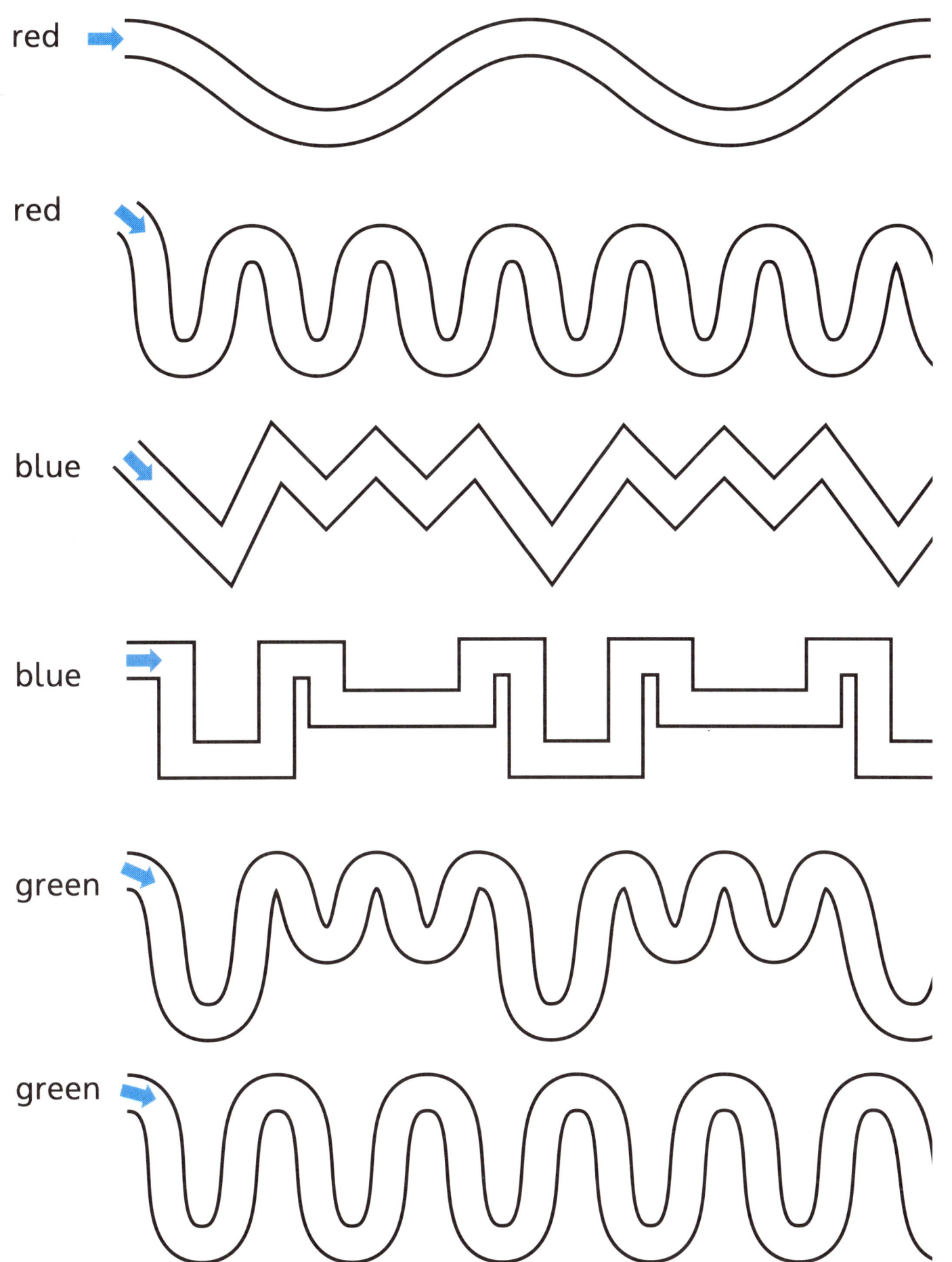

red

blue

green

yellow

orange

brown

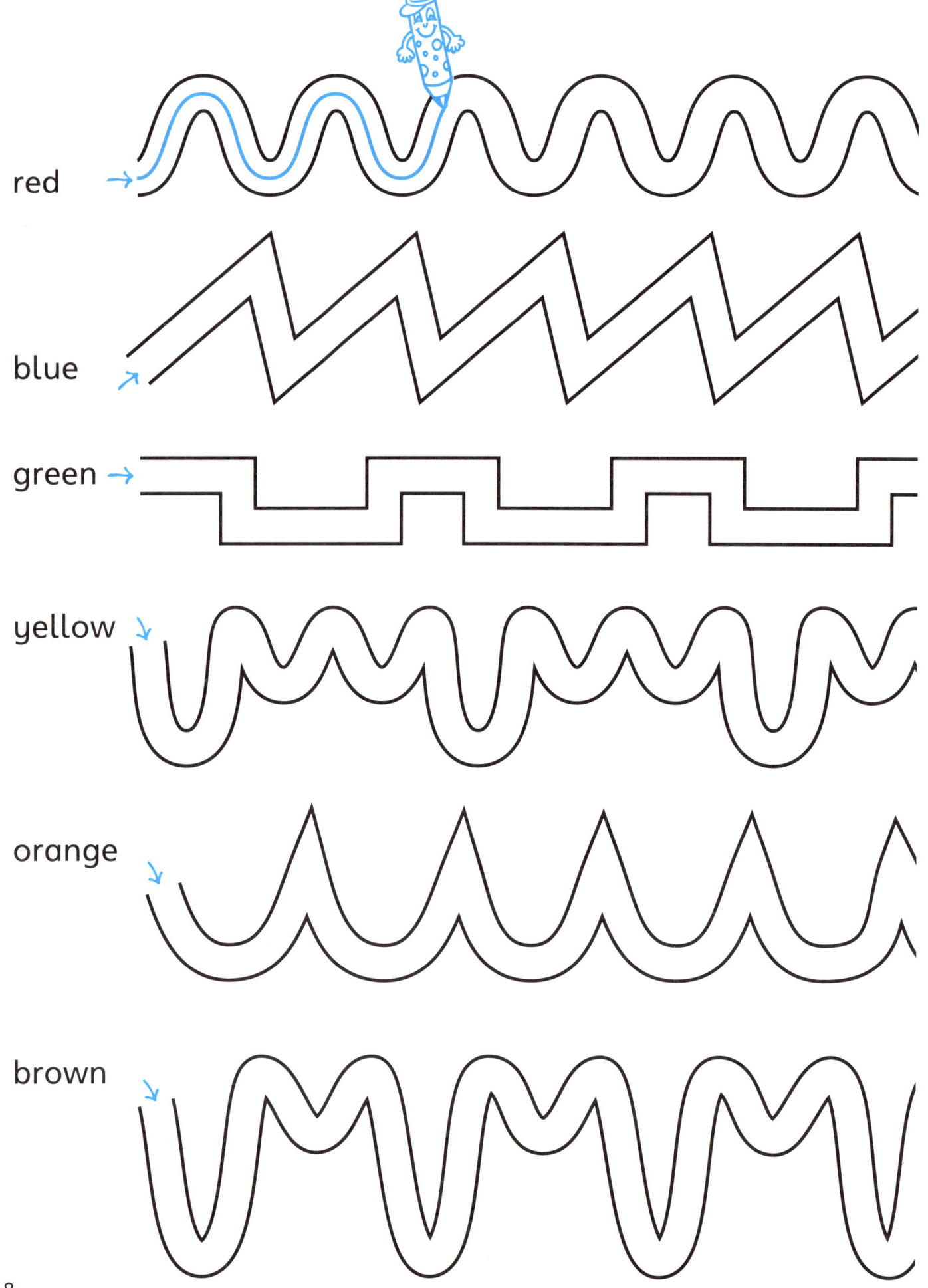

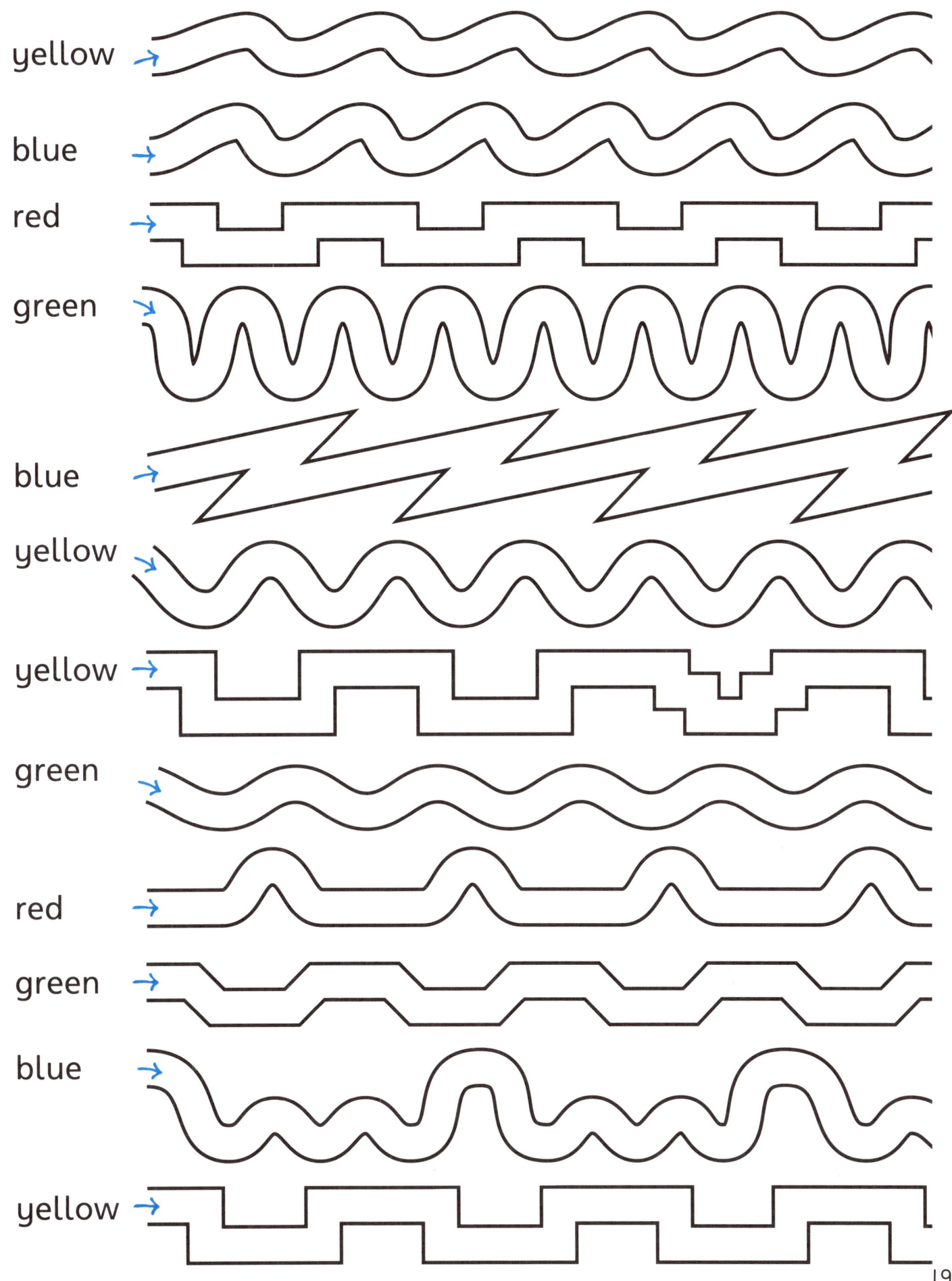

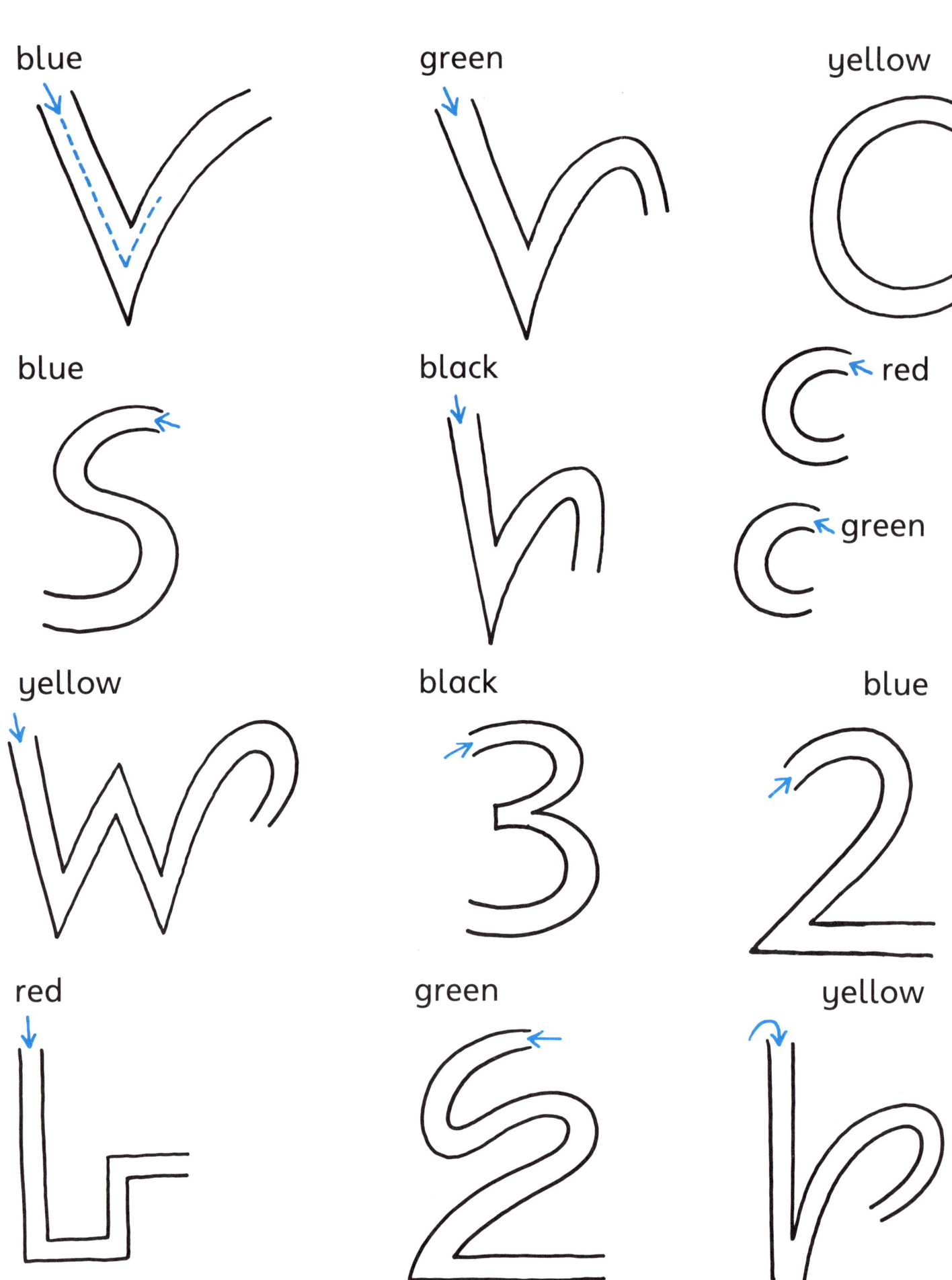

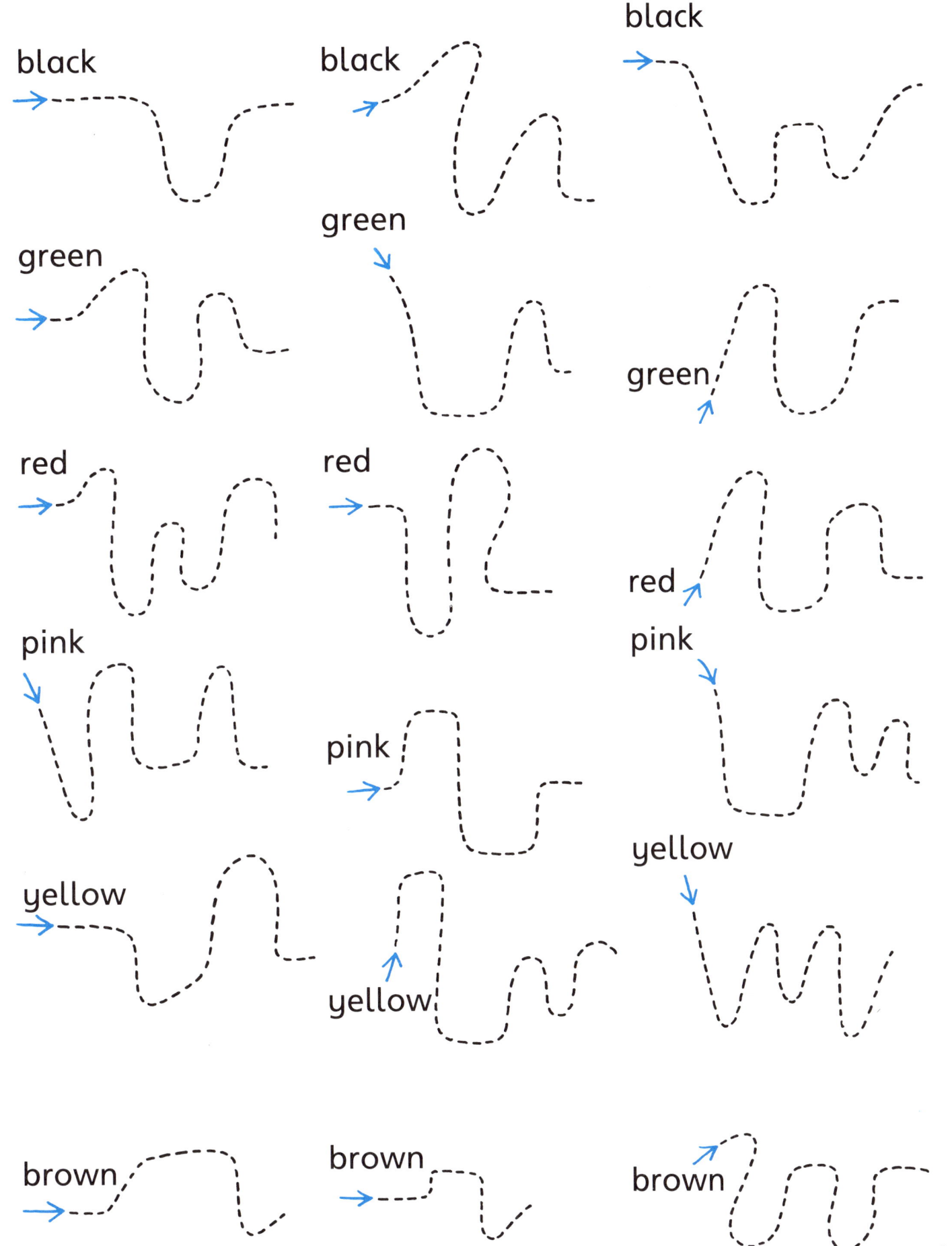

Do not go off the path!

Writing curves

Find C

Trace **c** with your finger.

Then write **c** over each **c** in the box.

What words begin with the letter **c**?

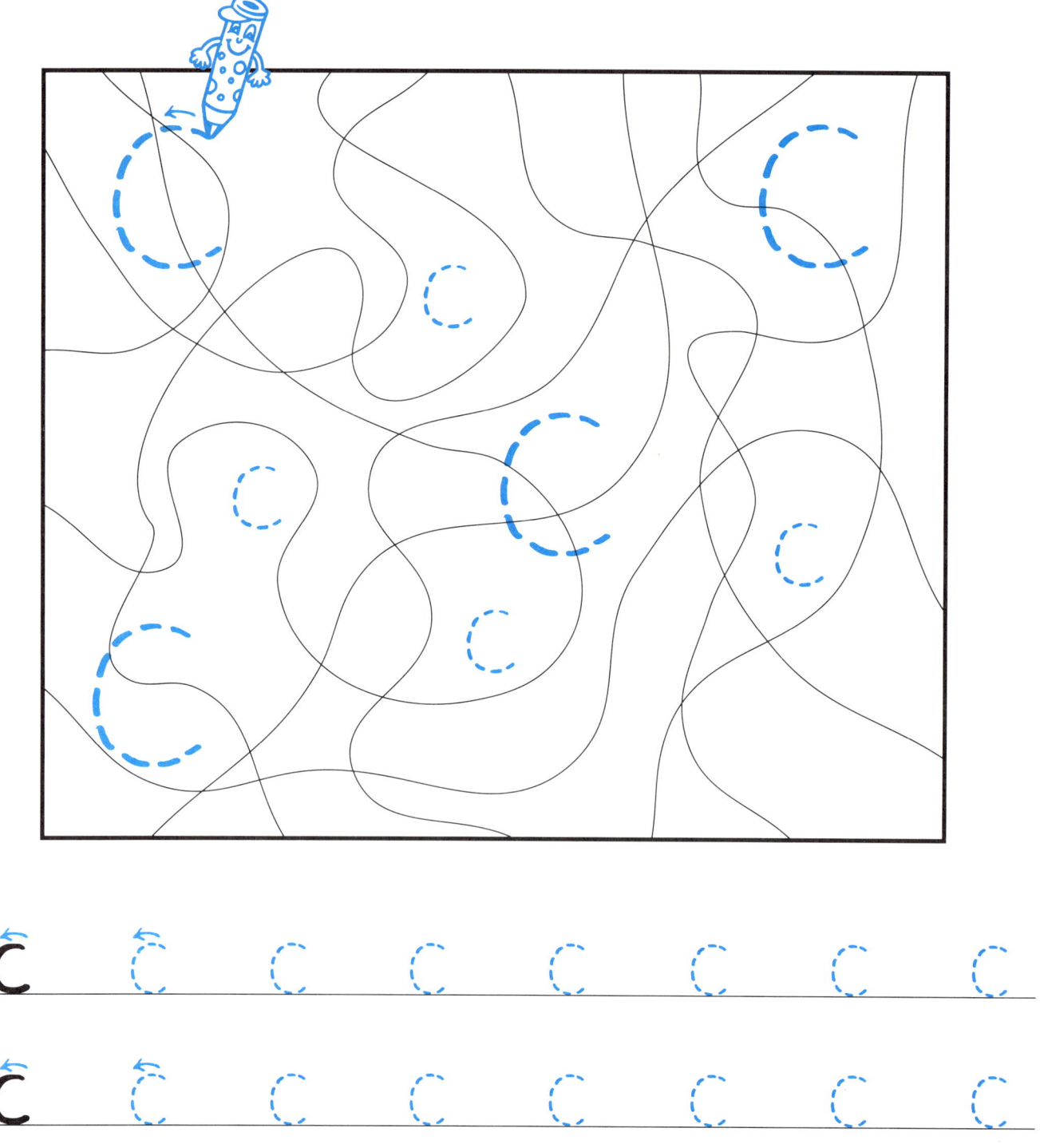

c

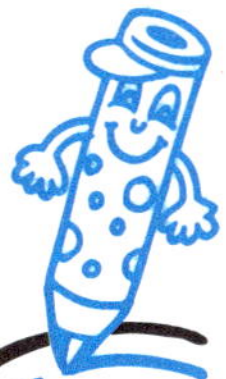

c c c c c

c c c c c

c c c c c c c c

c

cat

c

carrot

c

comb

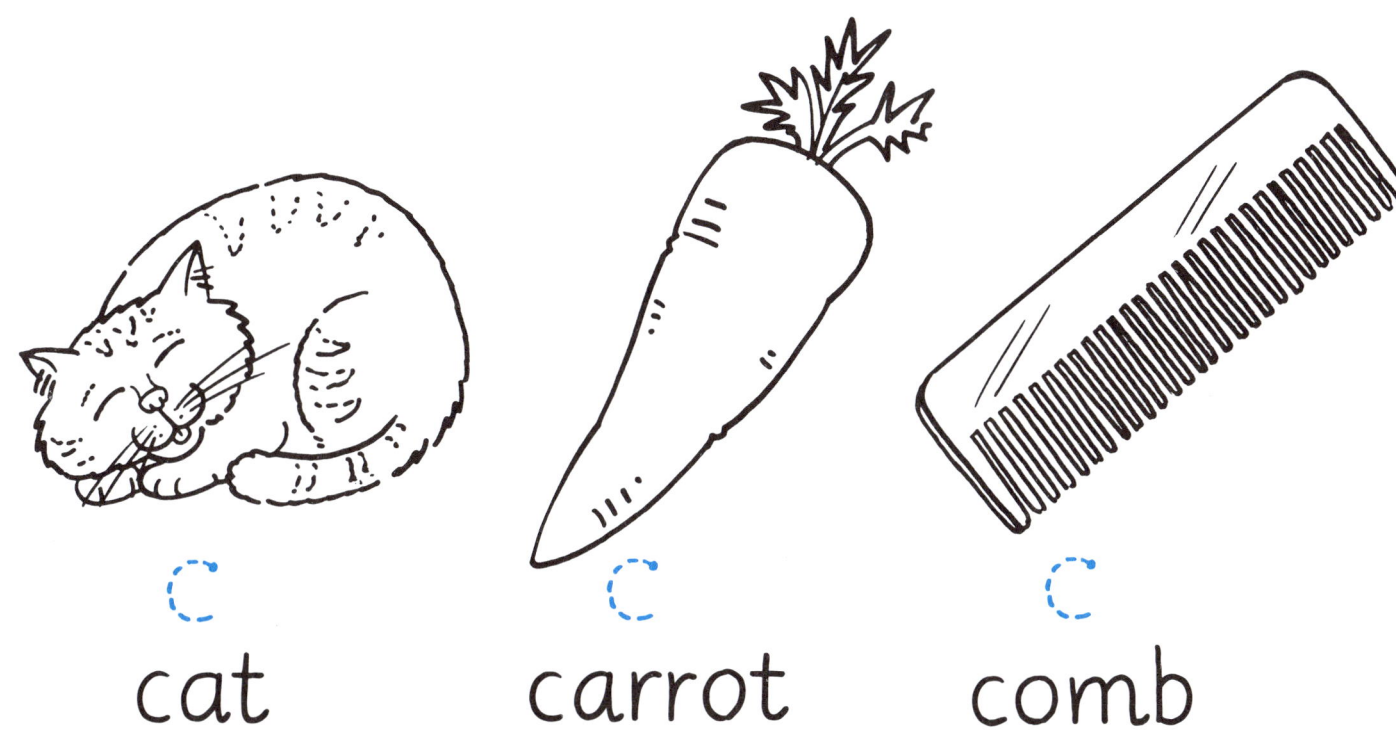

Find O

Trace **o** with your finger.

Then write **o** over each **o** in the box.

What words begin with the letter **o** ?

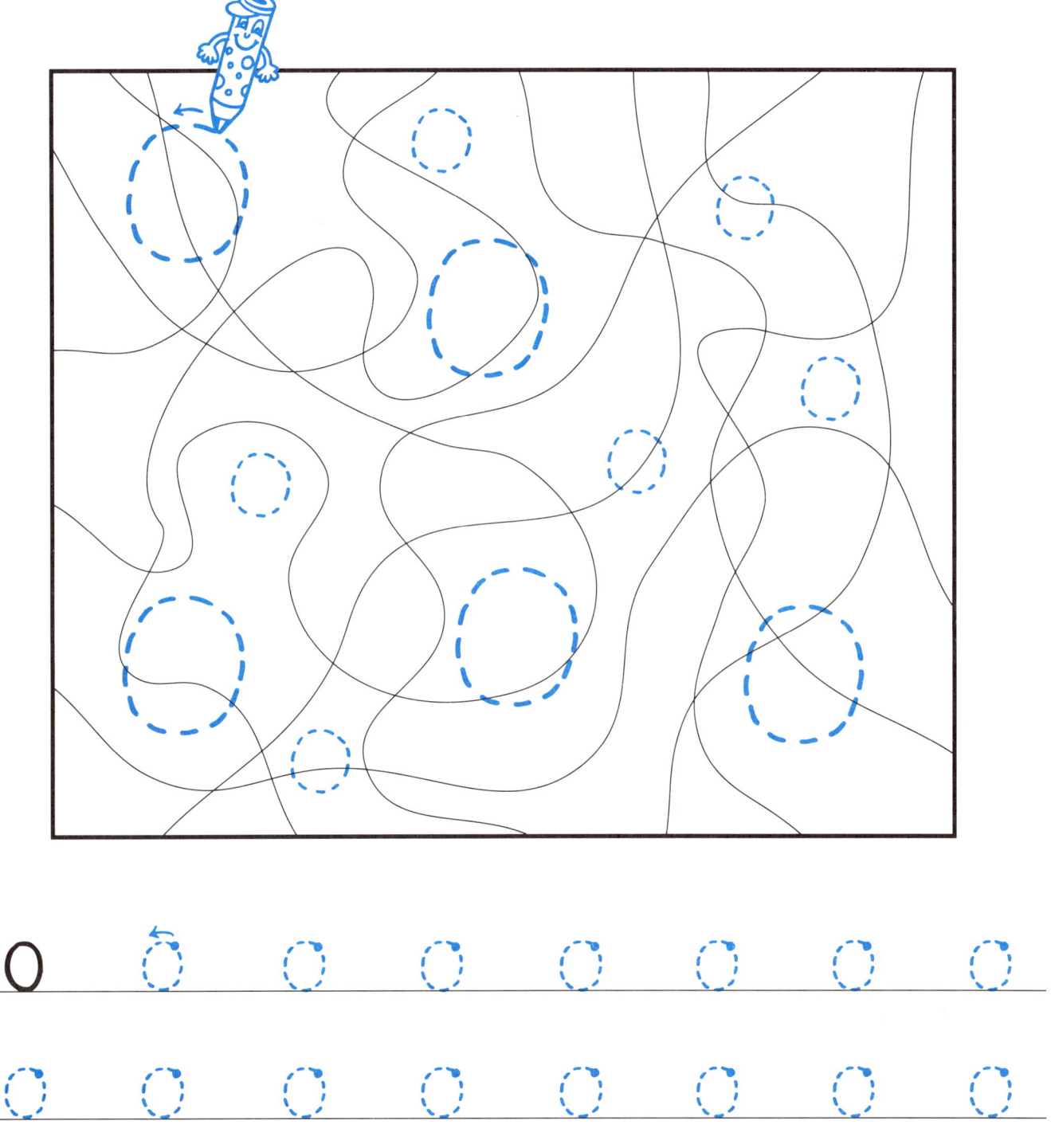

Find a

Trace **a** with your finger.

Then write **a** over each **a** in the box.

What words begin with the letter **a**?

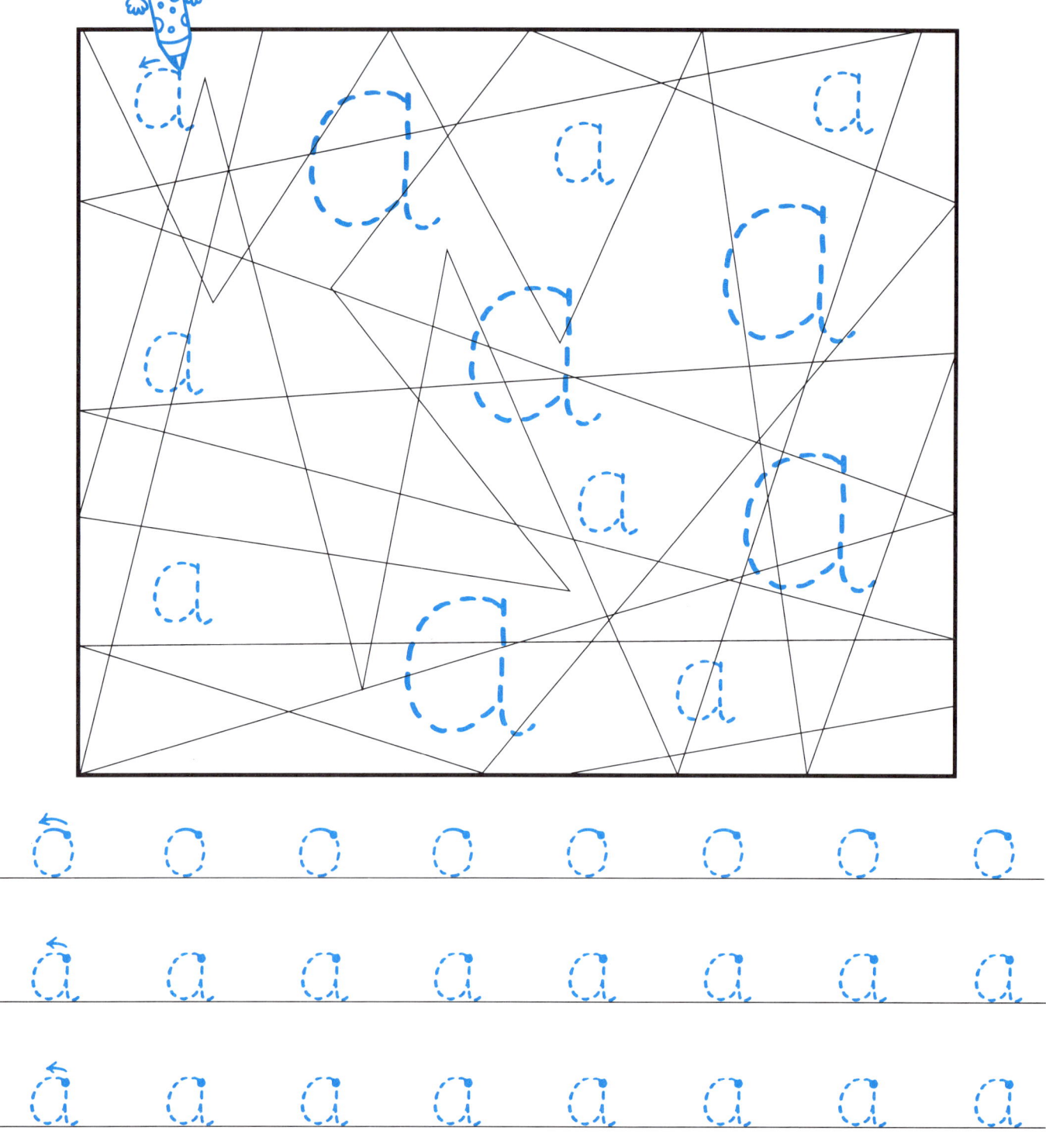

o a

Colour the **o** words black.
Colour the **a** words yellow.

c o a

c c c c c

o o o o o

a a a a a

Colour **c** shapes in blue.
Colour **o** shapes in yellow.
Colour **a** shapes in green.

c o d

c c c c c c c c

o o o o o o o o

d d d d d d d d

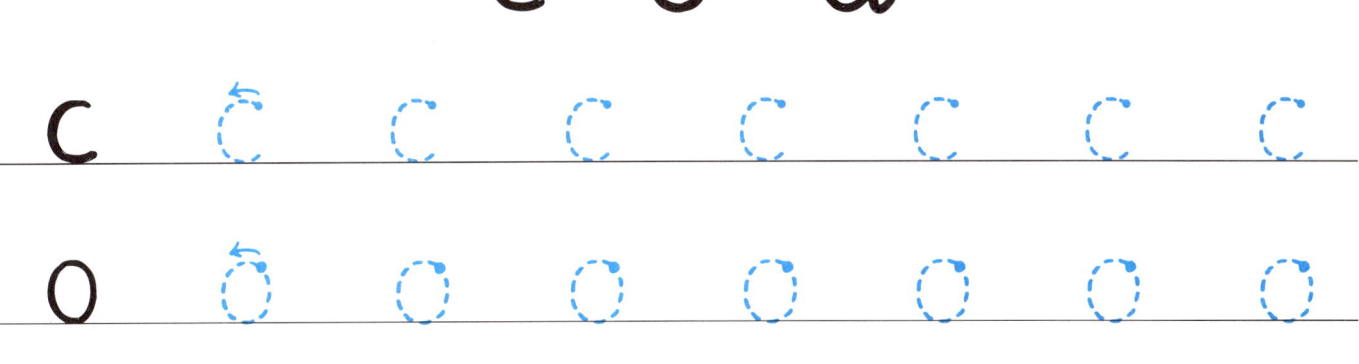

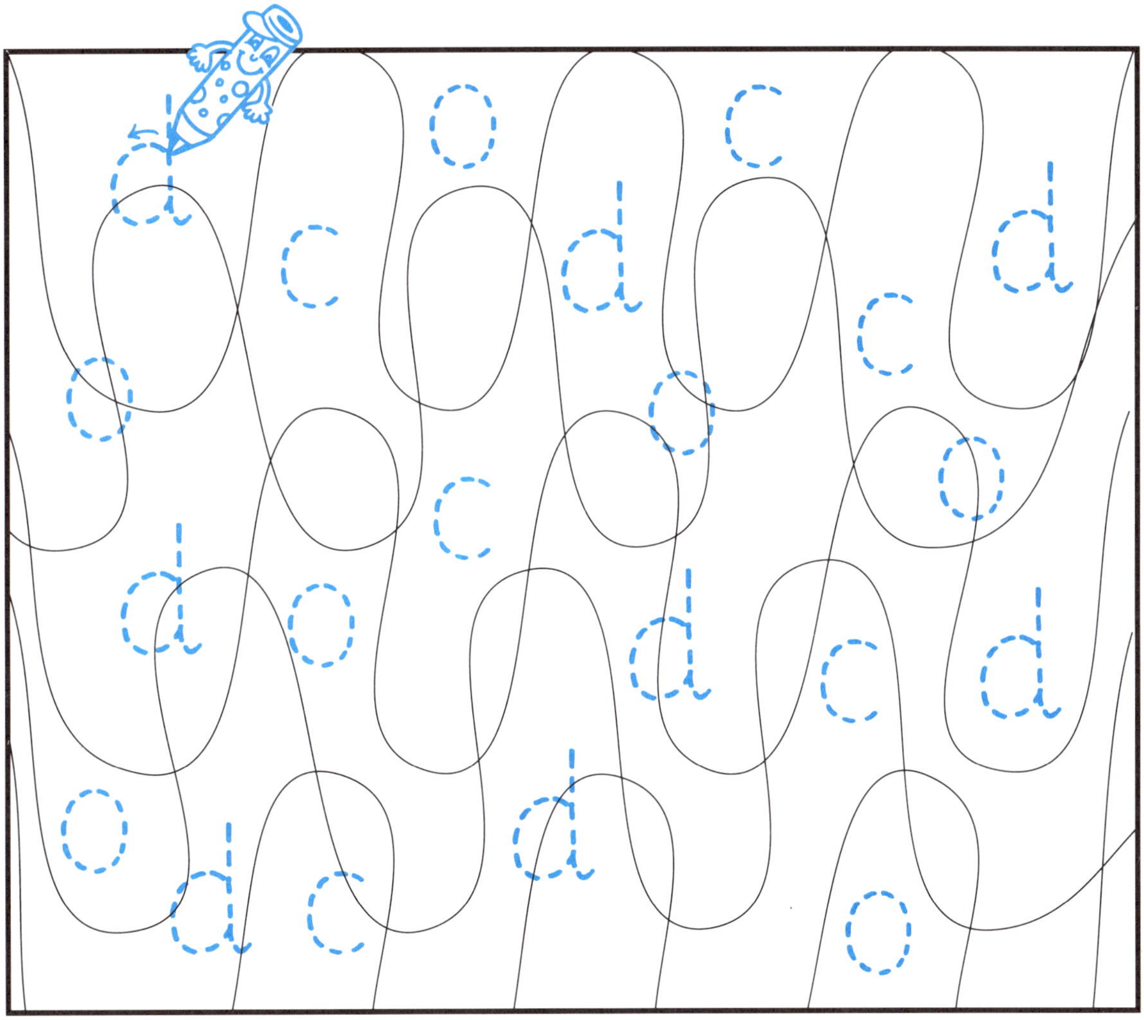

Write each **c** in blue.

Write each **o** in orange.

Write each **d** in green.

d

Write **d** under the things that begin with **d**.

r n

↓r ↓r r r r r r r

↓n ↓n n n n n n n

r   n

n   r

r   n

n   r

n   r

34

m

↓m ↓m m m m m

Write **m** under the things that begin with **m**.

r n m

↓r ↓r r r r

↓n ↓n n n n

↓m ↓m m m m

Colour

d in blue **r** in brown

n in green **m** in red

c

o

a

d

n

m

37

l t

Write l or t

2
t

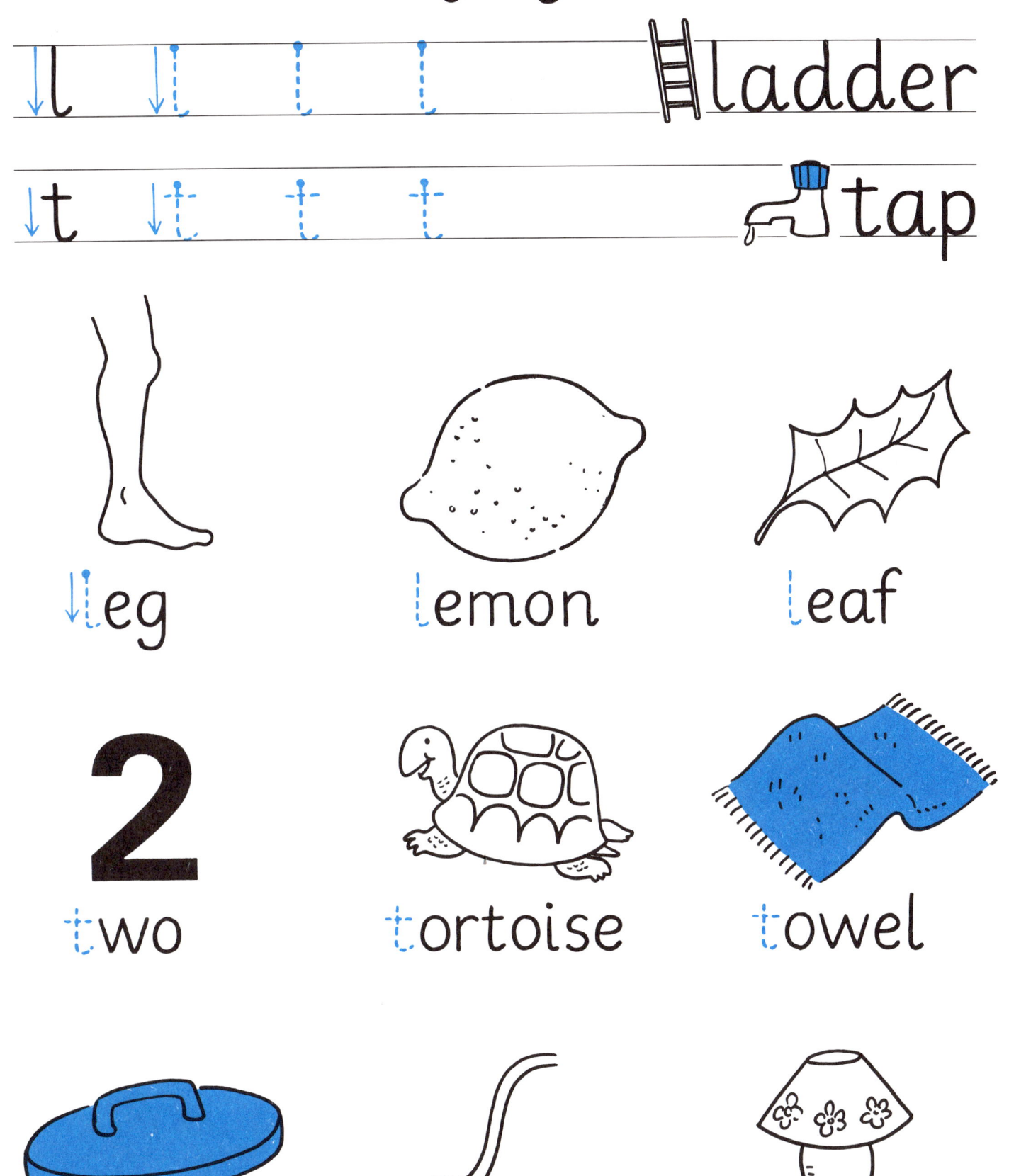

l t

l l l l ladder

t t t t tap

leg lemon leaf

two tortoise towel

lid tail lamp

s

steps

sock

6 six

spoon

saw

7 seven

skate

scissors

stamp

snake

sausages

spade

l t s

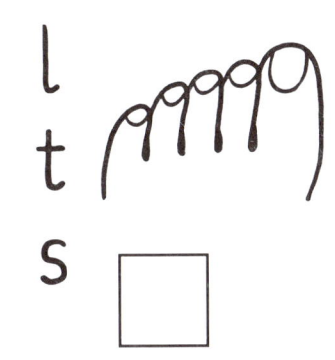

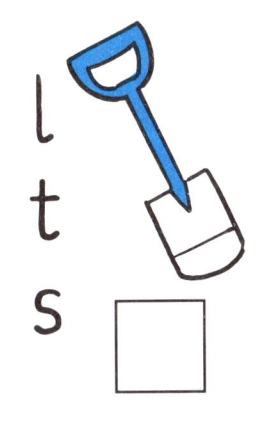

l l l   t t t   s s s

l t s	l t s	l t s
(sock)	(tap)	(toe)
l t s	l t s	l t s
(bear)	(snake)	(ladder)
l t s	l t s	l t s
(table)	(spade)	(stool)
l t s	l t s	l t s
(logs)	(tree)	(spoon)

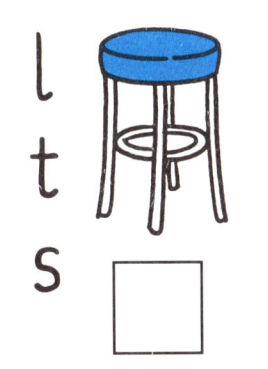

41

s h

s s s s s s s s

h h h h h h h h

Write s or h

s

_ _ _

_ _ _

_ _ _

42

This is me

My name is _____

I am _____ years old.

Next birthday I will be _____ years old.

I have _____ sisters.

I have _____ brothers.

Draw some hair

Draw 2 eyes

Draw 2 ears

Draw 1 nose

Draw 1 mouth

Draw 2 arms

Draw 2 legs

Draw 2 hands

Draw 2 feet

Draw some clothes on your drawing

Join the dots

Colour the dinosaur red.

Colour the T-shirt green.

Colour the jeans blue.

Colour the hair the colour you like best.

Colour the dog black.

Colour the dog's dinner brown.

The alphabet

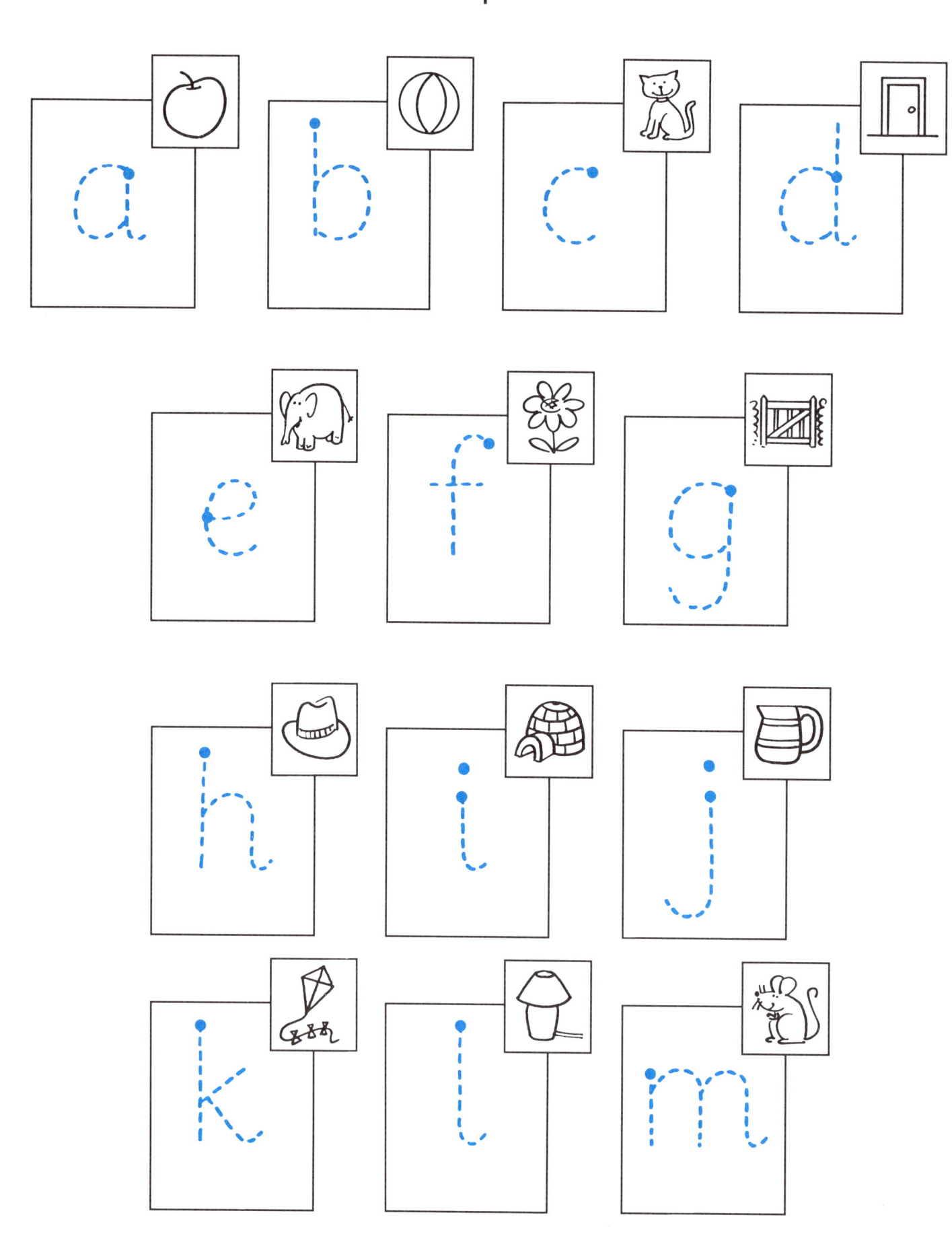

a b c d
e f g
h i j
k l m

n o p q

r s t

u v w

x y z

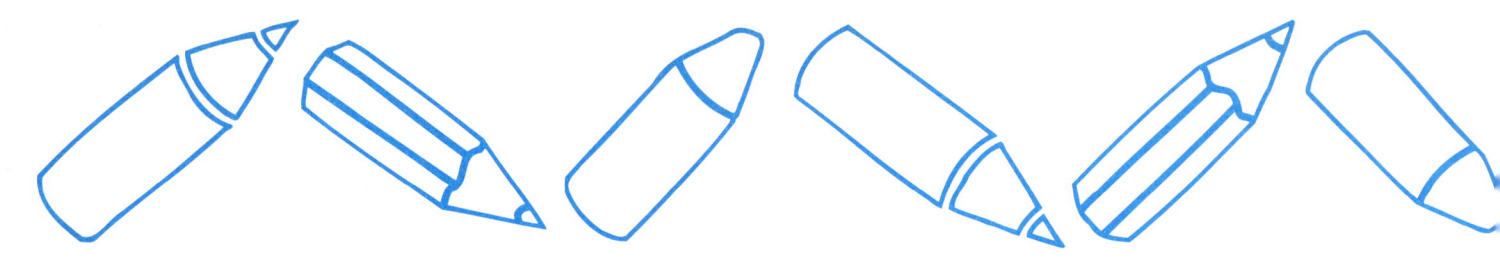

Notes for parents

This book falls into two sections.

pp. 4–23   The first part of the book practises 'writing pathways', i.e. drawing controlled lines along or between given tracks on the page. This obviously prepares the child for writing controlled and continuous letter shapes when they are ready to move on. Colouring in the pictures will also help the child's pencil control.

pp. 24–47   The second part of the book introduces individual letter forms in 'letter families', i.e. letters with similar shapes. The letter families introduced here are:

c, o, a, d
r, n, m
l, t
s and h

With each letter you should start by tracing the shape with the child's finger, then write the letter by starting at the dot and joining up the dotted line. Say the sound of the letter, and name words that begin with that letter.

These letters all end with 'exits', or hooks, to help the child's hand movement when they eventually progress to joined writing.

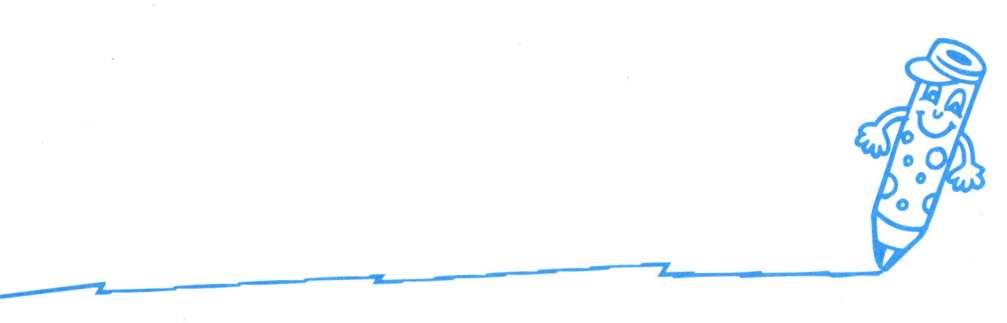

Oxford University Press, Walton Street, Oxford OX2 6DP
Oxford New York
Athens Auckland Bangkok Bombay
Calcutta Cape Town Dar es Salaam Delhi
Florence Hong Kong Istanbul Karachi
Kuala Lumpur Madras Madrid Melbourne
Mexico City Nairobi Paris Singapore
Taipei Tokyo Toronto

and associated companies in Berlin Ibadan

Oxford is a trade mark of Oxford University Press

© Jenny Ackland 1993
First published 1993
Reprinted 1993, 1994 (twice), 1995

ISBN 0 19 838116 6

Designed and Illustrated by Oxprint Ltd, Oxford
Printed in Hong Kong

All rights reserved. No part of this publication may be reproduced, stored in a retrieval system, or transmitted, in any form or by any means, without the prior permission in writing of Oxford University Press. Within the U.K., exceptions are allowed in respect of any fair dealing for the purpose of research or private study, or criticism or review, as permitted under the Copyright, Designs and Patents Act, 1988, or in the case of reprographic reproduction in accordance with the terms of licences issued by the Copyright Licensing Agency. Enquiries concerning reproduction outside those terms and in other countries should be sent to the Rights Department, Oxford University Press, at the address above.